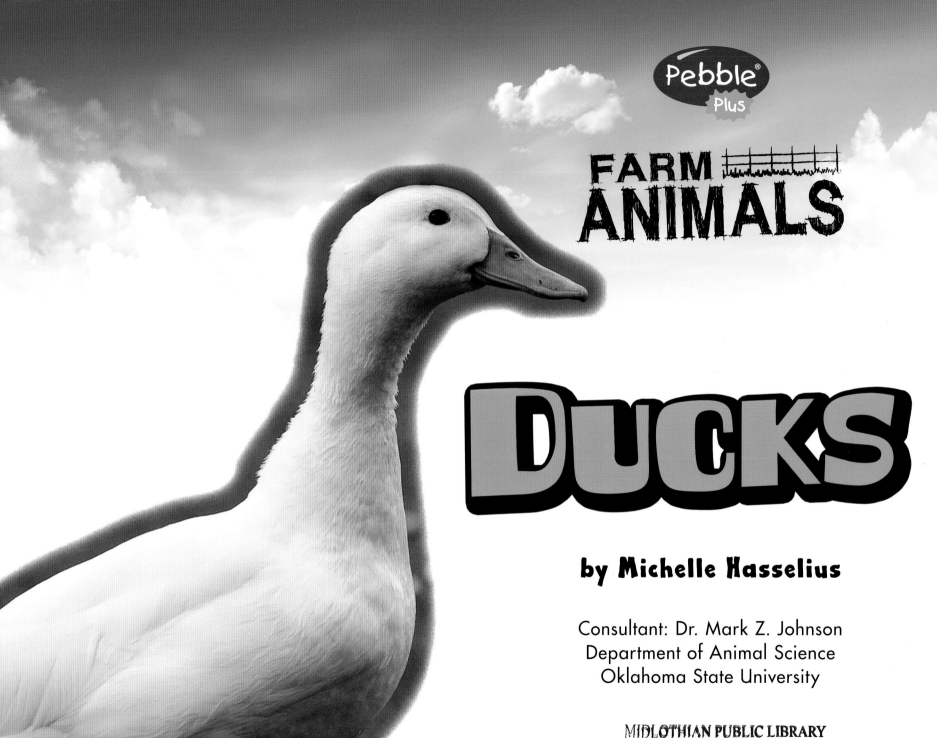

Pebble® Plus

FARM ANIMALS

DUCKS

by Michelle Hasselius

Consultant: Dr. Mark Z. Johnson
Department of Animal Science
Oklahoma State University

CAPSTONE PRESS
a capstone imprint

Pebble Plus is published by Capstone Press,
1710 Roe Crest Drive, North Mankato, Minnesota 56003.
www.mycapstone.com

Library of Congress Cataloging-in-Publication Data
Names: Hasselius, Michelle M., 1981– author.
Title: Ducks / by Michelle Hasselius.
Other titles: Pebble plus. Farm animals.
Description: North Mankato, Minnesota : Capstone Press, [2017] | Series:
Pebble plus. Farm animals. | Includes bibliographical references and index.
Identifiers: LCCN 2015049745
ISBN 9781515709268 (library binding) | ISBN 9781515709657 (pbk.) | ISBN 9781515711001 (ebook (pdf)
Subjects: LCSH: Ducks—Juvenile literature.
Classification: LCC SF505.3 .H37 2017 | DDC 636.5/97—dc23
LC record available at http://lccn.loc.gov/2015049745

Editorial Credits
Michelle Hasselius, editor; Kayla Rossow, designer; Pam Mitsakos, media researcher;
Katy LaVigne, production specialist

Photo Credits
Shutterstock: Alta Oosthuizen, 6–7, Catherine Murray, 21, Daniel-Alvarez, 18–19, Eky Studio (back cover background),
Elenamiv, 22 (background), Istvan Csak, 12–13, Jamie Rogers, 14–15, Kookkai_nak, 1 (background), kurt, 1, little_
stardust, 17, Mariia Golovianko, 9, originalpunkt, 5, OZMedia cover; Thinkstock: SmaliarIryna, 11

Note to Parents and Teachers

The Farm Animals series supports national science standards related to life science. This
book describes and illustrates ducks. The images support early readers in understanding
the text. The repetition of words and phrases helps early readers learn new words. This
book also introduces early readers to subject-specific vocabulary words, which are defined
in the Glossary section. Early readers may need assistance to read some words and to use
the Table of Contents, Glossary, Read More, Internet Sites, and Index sections of the book.

Printed and bound in China.
007708

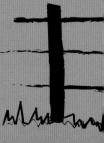

Table of Contents

Meet the Ducks

Quack! The ducks begin
their day on the farm.
Ducks swim in ponds
and streams. They waddle
across the grass.

Ducks have long feathers.
The outer feathers are
waterproof to help ducks
swim. The soft feathers
underneath keep them warm.

Ducks clean and straighten their feathers with their beaks.

More than 120 duck breeds
live around the world.
Only some live on farms.
Ducks can be white, black,
brown, or other colors.

Adults and Babies

Male and female ducks live on the farm. Males are called drakes. Females are called hens. Ducks can weigh 11 pounds (5 kilograms) or more. They live 2 to 12 years.

Baby ducks are called ducklings. Ducklings have soft, fluffy feathers called down. Ducklings walk and swim close together. It helps keep them safe from predators.

On the Farm

Farmers raise ducks for their meat and eggs. Hens start laying eggs in spring. Duck eggs are larger than chicken eggs.

Ducks spend most of their time
in water. They move their webbed
feet like paddles to swim.
Ducks can even swim in icy waters.
Their feet don't get cold.

Time to Eat

Ducks eat insects, plants, and seeds. To reach food underwater, farm ducks lift their tails high in the air. Their heads dip into the water to grab the food.

Predators such as foxes eat
ducks. Farmers build pens with
high fences to keep them out.
Ducks stay safe on the farm.

Glossary

breed—a certain kind of animal within an animal group

paddle—a short, wide oar used to move and steer some boats

pen—a small, fenced-in area for animals

predator—an animal that hunts other animals for food

underwater—under the surface of the water

waddle—to take short steps while moving from side to side

waterproof—able to keep water out

Read More

Andrews, Alexa. *On a Farm*. Penguin Young Readers. Level 1. New York: Penguin Young Readers, 2013.

Gibbs, Maddie. *Ducks*. Farmyard Friends. New York: PowerKids Press, 2015.

Nunn, Daniel. *Farm Animals: True or False?* True or False? Chicago: Capstone Raintree, 2013.

Internet Sites

FactHound offers a safe, fun way to find Internet sites related to this book. All of the sites on FactHound have been researched by our staff.

Here's all you do:

Visit *www.facthound.com*

Type in this code: 9781515709268

Super-cool stuff!

Check out projects, games and lots more at
www.capstonekids.com

Index